Nora Gracie Foster Presents

Bruno's Bedtime Roar

Bruno's Bedtime Roar
© 2025 Nora Gracie Foster. All rights reserved.

No part of this publication may be reproduced, distributed, or transmitted in any form or by any means, including photocopying, recording, or other electronic or mechanical methods, without the prior written permission of the publisher, except in the case of brief quotations embodied in critical reviews and certain other noncommercial uses permitted by copyright law.

First Edition: 2025
Designed by Stefania Grieco
Published by Stefania Grieco
Paperback ISBN: 978-1-998430-27-7
Hard Cover ISBN: 978-1-998430-28-4
eBook ISBN: 978-1-998430-26-0

Bruno's Best Friend Is...

....

(This Story Was Made Just for...)

Write your name or draw a picture of you and Bruno here!

Bruno sits in green pajamas on his round bed.

The moon shines like a silver coin.

Mama Bear stands by the door and says,

"Time for sleep."

Bruno roars.

He **stomps his paws** on the soft rug.

Papa Bear walks in.

The walls **shake** like tall trees in the wind.

Floppy falls from Bruno's paw.

Bruno picks him up
and **hugs him tight.**

The room smells warm,
like **fresh honey bread.**

Mama Bear kneels and says,
"Let's try step one."

Bruno sees her soft pink dress.

He feels air in his chest
like a big balloon.

Bruno **breathes in slow**
and lets it out.

The night air feels **cool** on his nose.

Floppy's scarf brushes his cheek
like **a cloud.**

Papa Bear smiles and says,
"Now step two."

The lamp glows **gold** in the corner.

Bruno **hugs Floppy**
and **feels safe.**

The **hug** makes Bruno's paws **warm**.

The bed feels like a big **soft hill**.

Mama Bear **hums** a gentle tune.

Papa Bear says,
"Step three is last."

Bruno looks at the **moon**.

It shines **bright**
like a **friendly face**.

Bruno thinks of **sunny fields**
with **tall grass.**

He sees **birds fly**
like **tiny arrows.**

Floppy's **button eyes**
seem to **smile.**

The room grows **quiet**
like **snow**.

Bruno's **roar is gone.**

Mama Bear **pats his head.**

Papa Bear sits by the bed
and tells a **short story**.

Bruno **listens** and **nods**.

The night feels
like a **soft blanket**.

Bruno **yawns**
and his **eyes close.**

Floppy **rests** under his chin.

The **moonlight** paints
silver shapes on the wall.

Mama Bear and Papa Bear
whisper good night.

The air smells **sweet,**
like **wild flowers.**

Bruno's **paws stop moving.**

Bruno **sleeps** with Floppy in his arms.

The house is **still.**

Bedtime feels like
the **best part** of the day.

Bruno **hugs Floppy**
and **shuts his eyes.**

Mama Bear said,
"**Sweet dreams, little bear.**"

The End

About the Author

Nora Gracie Foster is a children's author who loves turning everyday moments into magical adventures. Inspired by the beauty of Canada and the vibrant culture of Belize, she writes playful stories that spark curiosity, laughter, and a love for reading.

Her books are created for curious young readers (ages 3–12) and the grown-ups who read with them — combining imagination, learning, and lots of heart.

Nora believes that storytelling is a superpower — and every page is a chance to explore something new.

 Want to stay in touch or discover more fun adventures?
Look for her cheerful pencil mascot throughout her books!

🌙 Thank you

We hope you and your little one enjoyed the cozy bedtime journey of Bruno's Bedtime Roar.

If the story brought comfort, snuggles, or sleepy smiles, **please consider leaving a quick review** on Amazon.

Your kind words help other families discover the book and create peaceful moments of their own.

📱 Just scan below to leave a review — it only takes a moment, but it means the world.

❤️ With gratitude,

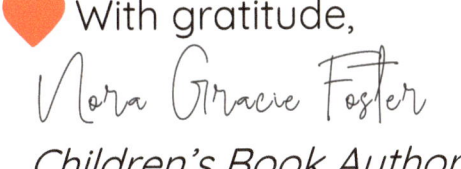

Children's Book Author

www.ingramcontent.com/pod-product-compliance
Lightning Source LLC
Chambersburg PA
CBHW041404010526
44107CB00015B/1071